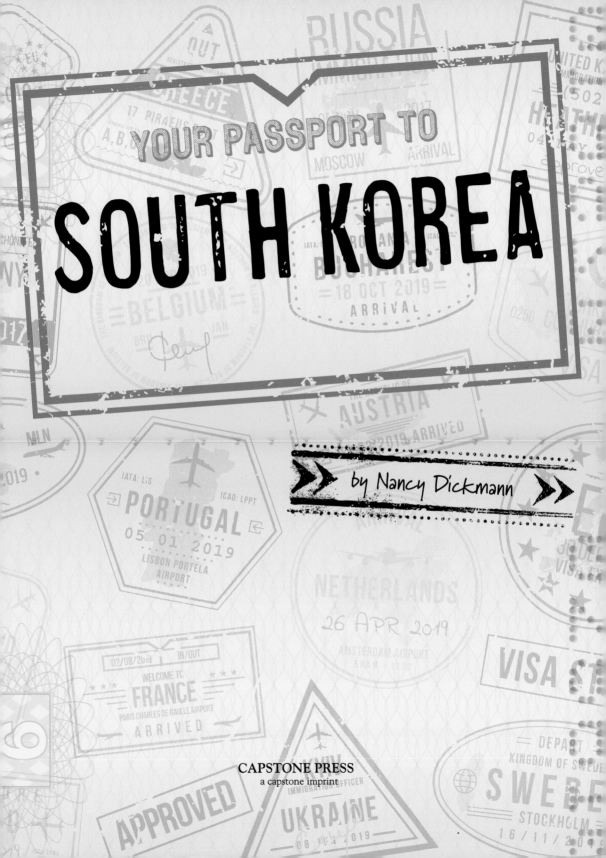

YOUR PASSPORT TO

SOUTH KOREA

by Nancy Dickmann

CAPSTONE PRESS
a capstone imprint

Capstone Captivate is published by Capstone Press, an imprint of Capstone.
1710 Roe Crest Drive
North Mankato, Minnesota 56003
www.capstonepub.com

Library of Congress Cataloging-in-Publication Data is available on the Library of Congress website.
ISBN: 978-1-4966-9553-6 (hardcover)
ISBN: 978-1-4966-9721-9 (paperback)
ISBN: 978-1-9771-5545-0 (eBook PDF)

Summary:
What would it be like to live in South Korea? How is South Korean culture unique? Explore the sights, traditions, and daily lives of people in South Korea.

Image Credits
Capstone: Eric Gohl, 5; Getty Images: JUNG YEON-JE, 20, VINCENT JANNINK, 29; Newscom: Pictures From History, 9; Shutterstock: anpanhel, 13, Dmitry Rukhlenko, Cover, FiledIMAGE, 14, Igor Grochev, 6, MYOUNG GYU KIM, 19, Noppasin Wongchum, 16, quiggyt4, 11, Subodh Agnihotri, 22, Suchart Boonyavech, 25, SUDONG KIM, 26

The publishers would like to thank Dr. Jieun Kim, School of Languages, Cultures, and Societies, University of Leeds, UK, for her help with this book.

Design Elements
iStockphoto: Yevhenii Dubinko; Shutterstock: admin_design, Flipser, MicroOne, Pavel Stasevich, pingebat

Editorial Credits
Editor: Clare Lewis; Designer: Juliette Peters; Media Research: Tracy Cummins; Premedia: Laura Manthe

CONTENTS

CHAPTER ONE
WELCOME TO SOUTH KOREA!.............................4

CHAPTER TWO
HISTORY OF SOUTH KOREA 8

CHAPTER THREE
EXPLORE SOUTH KOREA.............................12

CHAPTER FOUR
DAILY LIFE.............................18

CHAPTER FIVE
HOLIDAYS AND CELEBRATIONS 24

CHAPTER SIX
SPORTS AND RECREATION 28

GLOSSARY.............................30
READ MORE.............................31
INTERNET SITES 31
INDEX 32

Words in **bold** are in the glossary.

CHAPTER ONE

WELCOME TO SOUTH KOREA!

Skyscrapers reach toward the sky. There are neon signs lighting up the night. Shoppers crowd the streets. Young people are wearing trendy clothes and carrying the latest gadgets. The air is full of delicious smells. People buy tasty treats from street food stalls. It is a busy, bustling scene. This is Seoul, one of the world's most exciting cities. It is the capital of South Korea.

South Korea is a small country in the region of Korea in East Asia. North Korea is to the north. South Korea is about the size of Indiana. But many more people live there. South Korea is very densely populated. A lot of people are squeezed into a small space. But the country has beautiful wild spaces as well as cities.

MAP OF SOUTH KOREA

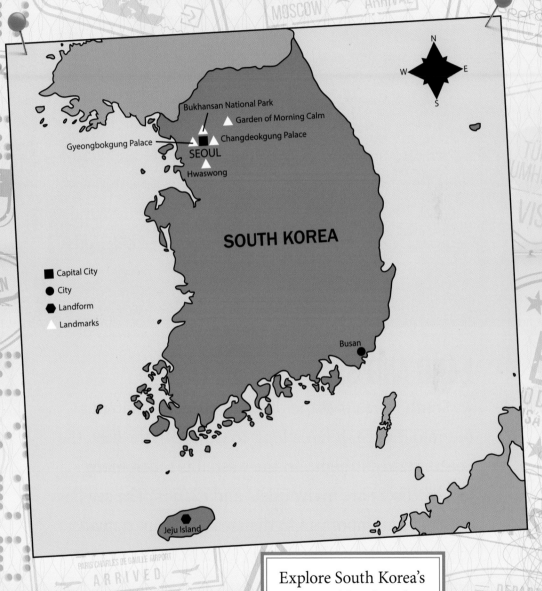

N
W E
S

Bukhansan National Park
Garden of Morning Calm
Gyeongbokgung Palace
Changdeokgung Palace
SEOUL
Hwaswong

SOUTH KOREA

■ Capital City
● City
⬡ Landform
▲ Landmarks

Busan

Jeju Island

Explore South Korea's
cities and landmarks.

The city of Busan is an important port.

LAND AND SEA

South Korea is at the tip of a **peninsula**, sticking out into the sea. It has a long coastline. In the east, the coast is fairly straight. In the west, it is much more jagged. There are many inlets and islands. The sea has always been important to the area. In the past, traders brought goods by ship. Today, it is one of the world's top shipbuilding nations.

FACT FILE

OFFICIAL NAME: .... REPUBLIC OF KOREA
POPULATION: 51,835,110
LAND AREA: .... 37,421 SQ. MI. (96,920 SQ KM)
CAPITAL: .... SEOUL
MONEY: .... WON
GOVERNMENT: .... PRESIDENTIAL REPUBLIC
LANGUAGE: .... KOREAN
GEOGRAPHY: South Korea's only land border is North Korea, to the north. The Yellow Sea is to the west and the East Sea (also known as the Sea of Japan) to the east. The Korea Strait separates it from the islands of Japan.
NATURAL RESOURCES: South Korea has wood, graphite, iron ore, and coal. It also grows rice, barley, and fruits and vegetables.

OLD AND NEW

South Korea has a long history. Many parts of its culture are very traditional. However, South Korea is also a modern country. It is famous for the high-tech products made there. They are sold around the world. It is also famous for its pop culture.

CHAPTER TWO

HISTORY OF SOUTH KOREA

One of the first kingdoms in Korea was called Gojoseon. It began more than 4,000 years ago. It started in the northern part of the peninsula. This kingdom collapsed about 2,000 years ago. Then a period called the Three Kingdoms began. Korea was divided into three separate kingdoms. Each had strong kings and large armies. They often fought with each other.

FACT

Legend says that a man called Dangun founded Gojoseon. His father was the god Hwanung. His mother was a bear who had turned into a woman.

ONE LAND, ONE KING

In 936 CE, a king called Wang Geon unified the entire peninsula. It was now a single kingdom. He called it Goryeo, which is where the name *Korea* comes from. But Korea's neighbor, China, was very powerful. Over the centuries China influenced Korea.

THE JOSEON DYNASTY

In 1392, a new dynasty began. It was called the Joseon Dynasty, and it replaced the Goryeo kingdom. This dynasty lasted for about 500 years. The capital was moved to Seoul. There were advances in science, and a new alphabet (Hangul) was developed for writing the Korean language.

TIMELINE OF SOUTH KOREAN HISTORY

2333 BCE: According to legend, Dangun founds the kingdom of Gojoseon.

57 BC: The Three Kingdoms period begins.

668 CE: One of the Three Kingdoms, Silla, conquered the other two kingdoms.

918: Wang Geon founds the kingdom of Goryeo and later unifies all of Korea.

1392: A new ruling dynasty, the Joseon, begins.

1592: The Korean navy fights off an invasion by Japan.

1656: The first European ship arrives in Korea and the crew is put in prison.

1910: Korea becomes a colony of Japan.

1945: At the end of World War II, Korea is split into North and South.

1948: Syngman Rhee is elected as the first president of the Republic of Korea.

1950–53: The Korean War is fought between North and South Korea and their supporters.

THE JAPANESE TAKE OVER

In the Joseon period, Korea was often under attack. The Japanese finally took over the country in 1910. The new rulers wanted to make Korea Japanese. People had to speak Japanese. They even had to change their names to Japanese ones. The Japanese built modern factories and power plants. They forced Koreans to work in them.

SPLIT IN TWO

Japan was defeated in World War II. In 1945, the **Allies** decided Korea's future. The peninsula was divided in half. The northern half was controlled by the **Soviet Union**. The United States controlled the southern half.

In 1950, soldiers from North Korea invaded South Korea. They were supported by China and the Soviet Union. Backed by the U.S. and other countries, the south fought back. This war lasted until 1953. The two countries are still divided. A thin strip of land separates them.

This sculpture honors the soldiers who fought against North Korea.

CHAPTER THREE

EXPLORE SOUTH KOREA

About 15 million tourists visit South Korea every year. The largest group comes from Japan. But people from all over the world tour this amazing country. Many of them explore South Korea's natural beauty. One of the most stunning sights is the island of Jeju. Long ago, it was an active **volcano**. Now, tourists hike and enjoy the beaches. Jeju once had its own kingdom, with a unique culture.

PARKS AND GARDENS

Bukhansan National Park is just north of Seoul. Visitors go there to escape the busy city. It gets more visitors than any other national park. It has pine forests and mountain peaks. There are hiking trails and places to go rock climbing.

Many movies have been filmed at the Garden of Morning Calm.

Gardens and nature are important in Korean culture. The Garden of Morning Calm is near Seoul. It has many different flowers, trees, and shrubs. It is beautiful in any season.

Tourists enjoy watching the changing of the guard ceremony at Gyeongbokgung Palace.

HISTORIC PALACES

Different kings ruled South Korea over the centuries. They have left behind grand palaces. Gyeongbokgung Palace was built around 1400. The city of Seoul has grown up around it. The palace has museums that tell its story. Changdeokgung Palace is a bit smaller. It has a beautiful garden and pond.

TEMPLES AND FORTRESSES

Buddhism has strong roots in South Korea. The country is dotted with beautiful Buddhist temples. Ssanggyesa is one of them. It was built about 1,300 years ago. It is a peaceful place, nestled at the foot of a mountain. In spring, the cherry trees burst into blossom.

People also visit the historic **fortress** of Hwaseong. It has guarded the city of Suwon since 1796. Its thick walls stretch for 3.5 miles (5.7 kilometers). In many places they are 33 feet (10 meters) high!

FACT

More than one million tourists visit the Korean Demilitarized Zone (DMZ) each year. This strip of land separates North and South Korea. There are fences and barbed wire. Soldiers guard both sides.

The busy city of Seoul is home to about 10 million people.

EXCITING CITIES

Most visitors to South Korea start their trip in Seoul. There are ancient palaces and modern skyscrapers. Some areas have narrow streets crammed with galleries, tea shops, and restaurants. There are also vast markets. Their stalls sell everything from hot food to traditional crafts.

Busan is South Korea's second-largest city. It is on the southeast coast. There are beaches and fish markets. There are also temples, and the area has many mountains.

BUKCHON HANOK VILLAGE

Many tourists visit Bukchon Hanok Village. This neighborhood is in the hills overlooking northern Seoul. Narrow streets are lined with traditional wooden houses. These *hanoks* are about 600 years old. Long ago, palace officials lived here. Now ordinary South Koreans do.

ENTERTAINMENT

Korean cities are full of things to do. In Korean, "bang" means "room." At a PC-bang, you can play computer games. In a manhwa-bang, you can read books or comics. A norae-bang is for singing karaoke. DVD-bangs are for watching movies. Many of these places also serve food.

CHAPTER FOUR

DAILY LIFE

There are very few **immigrants** in South Korea, though more arrive every year. Nearly 98 percent of people are Korean. There are small communities of people from Japan and China. People speak a language called Korean. It is slightly related to Japanese. It also has many words originally from Chinese.

FARMING

South Korea is a very urban country. Fewer than 20 percent of people live in the countryside. There are fishing villages near the coast. There are also villages high in the mountains. In the lowlands, farmers grow rice and raise animals. They also grow citrus fruits and cabbage.

FACT

In a South Korean name, the last name (family name) goes first. Some last names are very common. About half the country's population has one of the three most common last names: Kim, Park, or Lee.

People still wear hanbok for weddings, New Year celebrations, and funerals.

CLOTHING

Most people in Korea wear modern clothing. For special occasions, they wear traditional clothes called *hanbok*. This is a jacket worn with pants or a full skirt. Hanbok can be made of silk or cotton. It has bright colors and clean lines.

In South Korea, about two-thirds of students will go on to study at a university.

FAMILY LIFE

Family is very important in Korean life. People respect their older relatives. They look after them in old age. Education is also very important. Students are expected to work hard. Older children study for many hours a day.

CELEBRATING MILESTONES

Families celebrate important dates together. One of these is a baby's hundredth day of life. In the past, many babies did not live that long. For those who did, it was a time to celebrate. Parents would make offerings to the gods. People still invite friends and family and share rice cakes.

RELIGION

People in South Korea follow different religions. About one-quarter of people are Christian. Others follow traditional Asian religions. Some Koreans visit people called shamans. A shaman helps them contact the spirits. They can bring good luck or cure illness.

BATHING

Bathhouses are very popular in Korea. People come to relax and meet friends. A bathhouse has bathing pools at different temperatures. Some bathhouses, called jjimjil-bang, have hot, dry rooms and even restaurants.

KOREAN FOOD

South Korea is known for its tasty food. Most of it is very spicy! People usually eat with chopsticks. In some restaurants, diners sit cross-legged on floor cushions. Many dishes are for sharing with others at the table.

FAMOUS DISHES

The best-known Korean dish is probably kimchi. It is served as a side dish with many meals. It is a mix of vegetables, such as cabbage and radish. They are sliced and spices are added. Then everything is **fermented** to preserve it.

Many people buy side dishes of vegetables to take home and serve with rice.

For fast food, South Koreans turn to *ramyeon*. These instant noodles are quick and easy to prepare. They come in many different flavors. Bibimbap is also popular. This is a bowl of rice topped with vegetables. Meat and a fried egg are often added too.

PAJEON

These simple pancakes are often served as an appetizer or a side dish. They make a great snack too!

Ingredients:
- 1 bunch scallions
- 2 eggs
- 2 cups flour
- 1½ cups water
- salt
- 3 tbsp. oil
- soy sauce

Instructions:

1. Chop the scallions into 2-inch pieces. Use the white parts as well as the green parts.
2. Crack the eggs into a mixing bowl and beat them.
3. Add the flour, water, salt, and oil to the eggs and mix together. Then stir in the scallions.
4. Ask an adult to heat a frying pan and coat it with a little oil.
5. Pour in a scoop of batter. When it is golden brown on the bottom, flip it over to cook the other side.
6. Cut the pancakes into wedges and serve with soy sauce for dipping.

CHAPTER FIVE

HOLIDAYS AND CELEBRATIONS

South Koreans celebrate many different festivals. Seollal is one of the most important. It is the Korean new year. Seollal is based on the moon, so the date changes. It usually falls in late January or early February. Seollal is a three-day festival. People remember family members who have died. They share a meal that includes a special rice-cake soup. Then they give gifts and play games.

A celebration called Chuseok takes place in the fall. It is the harvest festival. People make special rice cakes filled with seeds, nuts, or beans. They are steamed over pine needles, giving the home a fresh scent.

Beautiful lanterns make the Buddha's birthday a colorful celebration.

FACT

South Koreans celebrate the Buddha's birthday in May. People parade through the streets carrying paper lanterns. Even people who are not Buddhist join in.

People travel from all over the world to celebrate the Boryeong mud festival.

NATURE FESTIVALS

Some South Korean festivals celebrate nature. In spring, the plum trees burst into bloom. Their sweet scent fills the air. People take picnics and sit among the trees to admire the blossoms.

In fall, the town of Muju holds a firefly festival. People come to see these glowing insects. The festival encourages people to protect the environment.

HAVING FUN

Dano is one of South Korea's oldest festivals. Today, people celebrate with music and theater. There are wrestling matches and swinging games. Women often wash their hair in sweet liquid.

The coastal town of Boryeong hosts a mud festival in July. The local mud has minerals that make it good for the skin. People come from all over to play in mud pits. There are mud fountains, slides, and races. No one goes home clean!

CHAPTER SIX

SPORTS AND RECREATION

South Koreans enjoy baseball and soccer. Fans watch their favorite teams play. The **martial art** of taekwondo began in Korea. Fighters kick, punch, and block. People all over the world now learn this sport. South Korean fighters have won many medals at the Olympics. South Korea also does well in archery and shooting.

The country's wrestlers win medals too. An older style of wrestling is also popular. It is called *ssireum*. It is similar to sumo. In this ancient sport, wrestlers hold on to each other's belts. They try to force their opponent to the ground.

FACT

South Korea is one of the few countries that have hosted both the Summer and Winter Olympics. The Summer Games were in Seoul in 1988. The Winter Games were in Pyeongchang in 2018.

28